SHARING THE GOOD NEWS

Stories Of Evangelism, Conversion and Baptism

The Word Among Us Press

9639 Doctor Perry Road

Ijamsville, Maryland 21754

ISBN: 0-932085-32-6

Cover design by Christopher Ranck

Made and printed in the United States of America.

Contents

Introduction

In the Acts of the Apostles, St. Luke paints a dynamic picture of the early church. What began with a few people on the day of Pentecost spread like fire throughout the world. In Jerusalem, thousands came to faith in Jesus. Later, as a result of persecution, Philip and other disciples preached wherever they were scattered—in Samaria, Antioch, Cyprus, and other places—and began to introduce Gentiles to faith in Christ. Then, Paul, Silas, and Barnabas spread the gospel throughout Asia and into Europe. As a result of these early evangelists, many others came to know Jesus and became servants of the gospel in their own right: Apollos, Timothy, Lydia, Aquila, Prisca, and many more.

What made these believers so eager to tell people about Jesus? Each of them experienced God's compelling love. They tasted the joy of knowing Jesus and longed to share that joy with everyone around them. Today, we too have been called to have just as deep an experience of

Jesus, something that will move us to proclaim the gospel as boldly and joyfully as they did.

There are many different ways to evangelize. We can reach out to someone who needs love. We can tell others how Jesus has changed our lives. We can pray with one who is sick or read a consoling Bible passage to one who is suffering. Or, we can simply be Jesus to others through generous service. We can bring Christ into every situation. We need not be ashamed of sharing about Jesus in gentleness and compassion. We can trust the Holy Spirit to lead us as we ask how we can share with our friends and relatives the love of Christ which has meant so much to us.

Many of us feel inadequate when it comes to speaking about Jesus. We need to understand that what matters is not our apparent success. Far more important are our love and obedience to Jesus. May the Lord anoint you with a deep desire to testify to his love and mercy demonstrated so beautifully at Calvary.

Jeff Smith
The Word Among Us

Coming To Know Jesus
Evangelism, Conversion, and Baptism

One night around the year 50 A.D., Paul and Silas were sitting in a prison in the city of Philippi. Earlier that day, they had been attacked and beaten by an angry mob, flogged at the command of the magistrates, and thrown into prison to await trial. Yet, even though they were in a great deal of pain, their spirits were high. They were not going to get depressed over all that had happened to them. Instead, Paul and

Silas rose above their suffering. Bruised and bloodied, yet filled with the Holy Spirit, they spent the night singing hymns and worshipping God in prayer.

The rest of the prisoners heard Paul and Silas and began to listen intently. Maybe they were enjoying the songs. Maybe they were thinking about the injustice that these two had endured, and the way they responded with joyful prayer. Perhaps they were reflecting on their own lives and wondering about their relationship with God.

Suddenly, in the midst of their prayer, the jail was shaken to its foundations. All the prison doors opened—as if on command—and everyone's chains came loose and fell to the ground. Here was a display of God's power for all to see. Two of his servants—badly wounded and cut off from all their friends—lifted their hearts to God in worship, and he moved in power. Everyone must have been awestruck by what they saw.

A Story of Conversion

Everyone, that is, except the jailer. Unlike the prisoners, he had chosen to go to sleep. The noise of the earthquake, however, was enough to wake him up and capture his interest. Roused from his sleep, he assessed the situation before him. With the doors opened, he assumed that all the prisoners had escaped. Surely he would be blamed, not only for their escape, but for the crimes they might commit now that they were on the loose. As far as he could tell, he had no choice but to kill himself.

But Paul intervened. "Do not harm yourself," he said. "We are all here" (Acts 16:28). Imagine that—not a single prisoner escaped! What's more, this suddenly desperate man was being reassured by one of

his prisoners. It must have been quite a picture—
Paul and Silas, bent under the pain of their
wounds, convincing a healthy, well-fed govern-
ment employee that his life was still worth living.

Whether it was the miracle of the earthquake,
or the fact that no one tried to escape, or Paul's
calm demeanor in a frightening situation, the
jailer knew he had come in touch with something supernatural. Paul had already "saved" him
from suicide, and now the jailer asked him how
he could be brought into a relationship with the
God whom Paul and Silas worshipped.

With simple directness, they replied, "Believe
in the Lord Jesus, and you will be saved" (Acts
16:31). He listened intently to the gospel that
these two men preached. Taking them into his
home, he tended their wounds and fed them a
meal. Then, accepting Jesus into his heart, he
and his whole family were baptized, "and he

rejoiced with all his household that he had believed in God" (16:34).

In this story of the Philippian jailer, St. Luke gives us a description of the way unbelievers joined the early church. For the first few centuries, the process was three-fold: evangelization, conversion, and then baptism. The order may be different today, *but all three elements remain essential: evangelization*—the sharing of the gospel; *conversion*—a decision to turn away from the world and to turn toward God; and *baptism*—the outpouring of God's grace to cleanse us from our sins and make us into children of God.

Evangelization

Evangelization is the sharing of the "good news" about Jesus Christ, the Son of God who saved us from our sins. On that night, the jailer witnessed the power of God in an unmistakable way. At first, the jailer had no interest in Paul and Silas—either in their sufferings or in their joyful praise and worship. However, after the prison doors were opened, his mind changed dramatically. Hearing that no one had escaped, he called for light. Little did he know that not only was he about to receive the physical light of a candle or a lantern; he would also receive the spiritual light of Jesus Christ.

The evangelization didn't end with the miraculous display of God's power. Paul and Silas "spoke the word of the Lord to him" (Acts 16:32). They told him about the death and resurrection of Jesus. They told him about God's love and about God's desire to free all people from sin and fill them with his life. They told him that he and his whole household could be forgiven and filled with the love of God.

Conversion

Conversion is the decision to turn away from sin and to turn to God. There are two dimensions of conversion—*initial conversion* and *ongoing conversion*. In Jesus' parable of the prodigal son, Luke gives us an image of both dimensions. Initial conversion is the primary decision to turn away from the world and to consecrate one's life to Christ. The prodigal son made his initial conversion when he "came to himself" (Luke 15:17) and returned to his father's house.

The boy's older brother, however, had already made the initial choice for his father, but he still needed to be freed from self-righteousness, anger, and resentment. His conversion needed to continue and deepen. God always wants to pour out his grace to protect us and free us from the sinful tendencies and motivations in our hearts.

He continually invites us to make decisions that will draw us closer to Jesus and turn us farther away from sin. Ongoing conversion depends on the grace we receive in prayer, through the sacraments, and through serving other people.

We can tell that the jailer experienced an initial conversion because he asked, "What must I do to be saved?" (Acts 16:30). He experienced a taste of heavenly reality, and that taste left him hungry for more. He knew he needed to be saved. He saw the peace and joy of Paul and Silas, and he wanted it for himself and his family.

Baptism

Baptism cleanses us of original sin, transforms us into a "new creation" (2 Corinthians 5:17), and incorporates us into the body of Christ (see *Catechism of the Catholic Church*, 1262-1270). Baptism supposes that a person has heard the gospel, has believed in Christ, and has confessed that Jesus is risen from the dead. In the case of infant baptism, it is assumed that the child's parents and godparents will undertake the primary responsibility of evangelizing the child and bringing him or her to a mature decision to turn from sin and turn to Christ.

After the jailer heard the gospel as preached by Paul and Silas, he "was baptized at once" (Acts 16:33). His conversion—his decision to live for Christ—was blessed and empowered by the grace of God through this sacrament. As a result of his baptism, he and his whole family were filled with joy over the mercy of God.

Conversion is a mysterious combination of our decision and God's all-powerful grace. We must choose to give our lives to Jesus, but we would not even be able to make such a choice if it were not for the Holy Spirit showing us our need for Christ and his great love for us. We need God's grace; we need the mercy poured out in baptism, the Eucharist, and the Sacrament of Reconciliation. Without the continual cleansing and nourishing power of these gifts, we would fall again and again.

Witnessing to the Gospel

As they prayed and sang songs of praise to Jesus that night, Paul and Silas gave witness to Jesus. Their demonstration of joyful suffering must have moved the other prisoners. We don't know exactly why, but we can assume that the Spirit was using these two apostles to touch the prisoners' hearts. Why else would they stay awake to listen to them pray and sing?

Paul and Silas also witnessed to the jailer. The jailer was evangelized by both the dramatic miracle and the witness of Paul and Silas. We know that he experienced an initial conversion because he asked, "What must I do to be saved?" Finally, Paul and Silas baptized the jailer and his whole family. Just as it was true for the early church, it is true for us today: Each of these three elements is crucial for every one of us. Evangelization, conversion, and baptism combine to bring a deep and lasting transformation in our hearts and in the hearts of those we care for.

The jailer probably remembered that night for the rest of his life. Far from being "just another quiet evening," it was the night that the Holy Spirit opened his heart to the gospel. It was the night that he met Jesus and experienced the forgiveness of his sins. Wouldn't you remember such a night?

Luke tells us that the jailer "rejoiced with all his household that he had believed in God" (Acts

16:34). God wants each one of us to be full of joy because we place our faith and our hope in Jesus, the author and perfecter of our faith. He wants us to witness to the gospel as well. He wants to empower all of us to bring the light of Christ to those in darkness.

A Chain Reaction
Evangelism, Conversion, and Baptism

What do you think would have happened that night if Paul and Silas had not been put into prison? Would the prison doors have opened? If the doors had opened, would the prisoners have stayed? Who would have given them the witness of loving prayer and joyful singing? Would the jailer have ever come to know the light of Christ? Would his family have been evangelized, converted, and baptized? How many people do you think were touched in later life by the witness of the prisoners or by the jailer or by a member of the jailer's family? Do you see the chain reaction? This is the way God works—he uses anyone who turns to him. The witness of just one of us can cause a chain reaction that brings the light of the gospel to a whole host of people.

Evangelization

The gospels tell us how Jesus evangelized people throughout his ministry: the twelve apostles; Mary, Martha, and their brother Lazarus; the woman at the well; the centurion; the blind man; and so many others. It all started when one man—Jesus of Nazareth—decided to share the good news of his Father's love. Then, immediately after the gospels, scripture gives us the Acts of the Apostles, a book filled with stories about people coming to know Jesus through the efforts of the first Christians. Throughout the book of Acts, we read how these disciples preached the gospel, healed people, and brought them to conversion.

Just like the first believers, we too have been given the authority of God from Christ himself. Jesus told us that we have the capability to do even greater things than he (John 14:12). We may think, "How can I do even a small portion of all that Jesus did? My faith is so small." However, if we all take small steps in faith, we will begin to discover how faithful Jesus is to his promises. There are many people in the world who need to hear the gospel. We have the Spirit—the presence and the power of God—within us. God calls us to use this power to lead people to Jesus. He calls us to be his instruments.

Through their prayers and singing, Paul and Silas led people to accept Jesus. Through the power of healing and casting out demons, the apostles also led people to Jesus. St. Luke tells us that Peter's preaching (Acts 2:14-41), the fellowship of the early church (2:42), the prayer of healing (3:6-10; 5:14-16), and the prayer meetings of the first Christians (2:44-47) were all effective in moving people to give their lives to Jesus.

Bearing Witness to Jesus

Scripture and church history show us that there are many different ways to evangelize people. Yet, even though the ways may vary, the goal is always the same: that people would come to know that Jesus is Lord, that he saved us from our sins, that Jesus loves every person, and that he has a loving plan for each one of us.

One man likes to recount the story of how he unknowingly evangelized his secretary.

Every morning at about 10:30, he would tell her, "Please—no calls or visitors for fifteen minutes. I don't want to be disturbed." One day, in a conversation with her, the man found out that his secretary knew he was a Christian. When he asked her how she knew, she said, "I could see the difference in your demeanor every day at about 10:45. When you come out of your office after your fifteen minutes of quiet, you are different. You're more peaceful and enthusiastic. You seem happier. I just knew it had to be God's grace that changed you."

Many of us lack the boldness of Paul and Silas. Yet, even as we lack courage, we can still witness to our friends and neighbors. Our willingness to serve, our kindness, our generosity, and our genuine care and love for them can all testify to the love of Christ within us.

As we pray, "Lord, give me more courage to

step out in your name," the Holy Spirit will open up doors for us to evangelize. Earlier in this century in England, there was a Protestant pastor named Smith Wigglesworth who loved to share his faith with others. As he walked down the street, Wigglesworth would pray quietly for everyone he saw. Sometimes, his prayers were answered and, out of the blue, someone would come up to him and ask him for help. As a result, he led some to conversion. If God was able to do it for Smith Wigglesworth, he can do the same for us as well.

The witness of a warm, friendly, and caring parish will also attract people. Pastors who make eye contact and open the Mass with a warm greeting will bear a moving witness. If we all pray during Mass for people to experience conversion, we would see it happen. Paul and Silas are proof that prayer works as a means to evangelize. After Mass, we can take a moment and look around for someone we don't know. We can make it a point to go over and introduce ourselves with a warm and friendly smile. Positive first impressions like these can open doors that might otherwise remain shut.

Prayer and Evangelization

St. Bernard of Clairvaux felt that unless he experienced God's love, he could not speak about God and he could not encourage others to seek God. Bernard's writings—especially his *Sermons on the Song of Songs*—confirm that he found God and that he had indeed come to know the love of God. Because he had spent time in prayer allowing Jesus to win his heart, Bernard could bring others to know the love of God that had so filled him. How vital it is that we all stay close to Jesus!

Would Paul and Silas have been able to keep every prisoner awake if they had simply lectured them all about their sins and complained about how their own imprisonment was unjust? Wasn't it their love for Jesus that attracted the prisoners and the jailer? Our lack of courage may well be a stumbling block. However, whether or not we are courageous, our ongoing conversion, our closeness to Jesus, is a far more important issue.

Evangelization is not supposed to be a chore or a job we have to do. Evangelization is a mission we should want to do. Someone evangelized us. Was it a priest? A parent? A teacher? A fellow student? A friend at work? Was it Paul and Silas? Without that someone, where would we be in our faith? Wasn't that person a prayerful person? Wasn't it the witness of his or her love for

Jesus that attracted us?

We are going to be willing to evangelize others as we ourselves experience the love and joy of Jesus through the power of the Holy Spirit. Then, we will have the urge to evangelize. We will want others to come to know what we know—that Jesus is Lord, that he loves us, and that he has forgiven us. Like the person who sold everything to buy the field, or like the merchant who sold everything to buy the fine pearl (Matthew 13:44-46), we too will want to help people change their lives so they might know what we know—that Jesus, who is God, loves us.

The Harvesters Are Few

Many people have been baptized but may not be enjoying the fullness of their baptismal gift. Just as in the early church, people today need to experience conversion if they want to grasp all that they received at baptism. Some people are fortunate enough to experience conversion on their own—maybe through a vivid experience like St. Paul, or through an adverse experience such as sickness or financial trial. However, for most people, the experience of conversion is linked to the efforts of another Christian who, in some way, reaches out and touches them. For this to happen, there has to be someone willing to reach out. If that someone is going to be you or I, we will need to continue to grow closer to Jesus and we will have to try, with the help of the Holy Spirit, to step out and evangelize others.

Jesus told his disciples, "The harvest is plentiful, but the laborers are few" (Matthew 9:37). Let us all take a moment to ask Jesus for the courage to evangelize. Let us all ask Jesus to reveal himself more fully so that we would be drawn closer to him and our desire to evangelize would increase. Remember: Jesus is with you at every moment. He knows what is going on. He wants to give us everything we need to reap a full harvest.

Who knows? Maybe we will be called to sing and praise God and evangelize others, just like Paul and Silas—maybe even in prison!

Conversion in the
Gospel of Luke

In his gospel, and in his Acts of the Apostles, St. Luke loves to tell stories about how God empowers people to experience a deep conversion—to repent of their sins, change their lives, and believe in Jesus Christ. Think of all the vivid characters and situations Luke conveys in his works: the sinful woman (Luke 7:36-50), Zacchaeus (19:1-10), the "good thief" (23:39-43), the Ethiopian eunuch (Acts 8:26-40), Cornelius (Acts 10:1-48), and St. Paul himself (Acts 9,22,26). By prayerfully studying some of these stories, we can come to understand that conversion is not something that we do alone, but something that we do with God's help and direction.

John the Baptist and Conversion

In the beginning of Luke's Gospel, we read John the Baptist's challenging words: "You brood of vipers! Who warned you to flee from the wrath to come? Bear fruits that befit repentance" (Luke 3:7-8). In his preaching, John showed that a major motivation for conversion comes from the prophetic announcement of the wrath of God. "Wrath" is God's just judgment on sinners, and John called people to acknowledge their sin and to change their hearts and actions.

When the crowd asked him what they should do, John enumerated some of the fruits of repentance: Those who have should share with those who have not (Luke 3:10-11). Tax collectors should perform their required tasks justly (3:12-13). Soldiers should not extort money through threats and intimidation (3:14). John's call to conversion was a call to live the moral life by hearing the cry of the poor and being just in all our dealings.

For John, conversion entailed an honest appraisal of the sin in our lives. John showed that conversion also implied action—that we do things differently. This action itself can transform us. Sharing our goods makes us more aware of the people around us and helps us to see the generosity and goodness within our own hearts.

Jesus' Call to Conversion

Like John before him, Jesus also called people to repent: "The time is fulfilled, and the kingdom of God is at hand; repent, and believe in the gospel" (Mark 1:15). Also like John, Jesus was not above using dire warnings to those who would hear him: "Woe to you, Chorazin! Woe to you, Bethsaida! For if the mighty works done in you had been done in Tyre and Sidon, they would have repented long ago, sitting in sackcloth and ashes" (Luke 10:13).

Yet we can also notice a clear difference between John's strategy and Jesus' strategy. John waited for people to come to him to experience his baptism for the forgiveness of sins. Jesus went out and associated with sinners so that they could experience God's forgiveness and healing power in their own environments. Jesus, more than John, emphasized that conversion was not an action but a response, a response to God's initiative. When we read the different conversion stories in Luke and Acts, we are struck by how often it is God or Jesus—not the penitent—who takes the first step.

Both the Gospel of Luke and Acts are filled with conversion stories. Let's take a look at some to gain a deeper understanding of conversion and to see if any of them reflect our own experiences.

The Sinful Woman (Luke 7:36-50)

The story of the sinful woman is one of the most moving stories Luke tells, yet it is a story that we might misinterpret if we focus on what the woman has done rather than on what God has done. The woman did not earn forgiveness by her actions; rather her action was evidence that she had already experienced God's forgiveness. Jesus' response brings out this point clearly: "Her sins, which were many, have been forgiven; hence she has shown great love. But the one to whom little is forgiven, loves little" (Luke 7:47).

It was this woman's experience of forgiveness that empowered her to show Jesus such love. She was the great debtor in Jesus' parable whose entire debt was canceled (Luke 7:41-43), and such an act of mercy prompted her outpouring of love. This story shows that conversion is a response to God's action. We do not need to earn God's love and forgiveness. It is given to us as God's overflowing gift. Our conversion is simply a response to this great gift of God's love and mercy.

The "Prodigal Father" (Luke 15:11-32)

A key parable about conversion—found only in the Gospel of Luke—is the story of the prodigal son. When we read this parable, we often focus our attention on the son(s) instead of on the father. But a better title for this would be the "Prodigal Father." It is the boys' father who went to extremes—even bringing ridicule and shame upon himself—in his dealings with his two sons. According to the social values of Jesus' time, the father actually dishonored himself by going out to his sons instead of waiting for them to come to him (vv. 20, 28). So great—even prodigal—was his forgiveness that he put aside concern for his image in order to win his children back to himself.

By telling this story, Jesus proclaims that God is the prodigal father. Conversion for both of these sons is meant to be a response to what God our Father has done. Conversion is the process of recognizing our sin and allowing ourselves to be touched—even overwhelmed—by the love and mercy of God.

St. Paul—A Conversion and a Call
(Acts 9,22,26)

One of the central characters in Luke's second volume—Acts of the Apostles—is Paul, the zealous persecutor of the church who became a zealous missionary. Paul's encounter with the risen Lord on the road to Damascus worked a profound transformation in his life. This conversion story was so important for Luke that he recounted it three times: (1) a narrative account in Acts 9; (2) Paul's defense before the Jews in Acts 22; and (3) Paul's defense before the Roman ruler Festus and the Jewish King Agrippa in Acts 26.

In these various accounts, it seems as if Luke is giving an almost classic definition of conversion: Conversion means being knocked off of one's "high horse," which leads to a change in life. However, if we study these accounts in Luke, we may see some surprising challenges to this notion First of all, there is no mention of Paul being knocked off of a horse. Luke only tell us that Paul "fell to the ground" when a bright light flashed around him (Acts 9:4).

Even more importantly, Paul's transformation was not a conversion in the classic sense of turning away from idolatry (see 1 Thessalonians 1:9). As a devout Jew, Paul already worshipped the one true God. Nor was his conversion a change from an immoral and sinful life. Indeed, he told the Philippians that he was a good and righteous Jew: "as to righteousness under the law, blameless" (Philippians 3:6). Something more profound was going on—something that changed the very foundations of his life.

Paul did experience a transformation: God had predestined Paul, set him apart before he was born, and called him to proclaim the gospel among the Gentiles. When Paul describes this experience, he doesn't refer to it as a conversion, but as a call (Galatians 1:15-16; see Jeremiah 1:5). This experience vastly changed Paul: "Whatever gain I had, I counted as loss for the sake of Christ. Indeed I count everything as loss because of the surpassing worth of knowing Christ Jesus my Lord. For his sake I have suffered the loss of all things, and count them as refuse, in order that I may gain Christ" (Philippians 3:7-8).

Paul's encounter with the Lord reveals a wider meaning of conversion. It is not only a call away from sin and to the one true God. Conversion is also a call to mission, whether it be as a homemaker, an executive, a laborer, or a parent. Whatever our situation, God has called us and empowered us to proclaim the gospel in word and deed. We are not only called to change our lives, but to proclaim the gospel and bring others into the light of Christ as well.

Trusting in God

Throughout our lives, we are all called to live a continual process of conversion. As Luke makes clear over and over again, conversion is first of all about what God has done and is doing in our lives. Conversion is a response to God's activity in our lives. It is an acknowledgment of our sinfulness, and it is an acknowledgment of our deep need for God. Ultimately, conversion means trusting in God and going wherever he may lead us. We are truly converted when we pray as Jesus prayed: "Thy will be done" (Luke 22:42).

Empowered
To Be Witnesses

St. Paul once wrote: "We have this trea-
sure in earthen vessels, to show that the
transcendent power belongs to God, and
not to us" (2 Corinthians 4:7). During his
years as an evangelist, Paul came to understand that all of his education, eloquence,
and shrewdness were nothing compared
with the power of God within him. Rather
than trying to be a convincing philosopher
or a powerful orator, Paul learned that simply
by speaking the gospel in love and letting
God move in power, he was able to touch
people far more deeply.

Do you believe the same to be true for yourself? Do you know that, through baptism, you have the Holy Spirit living inside of you? Do you know that you have been empowered by God to bring the gospel to those around you? You don't have to be a deep theologian or a polished speaker. You only have to draw ever closer to Jesus and take small steps of faith in witnessing to the love of God. The smallest things done in love can begin a chain reaction that touches an amazing number of people. All God asks is that we love him, obey him, and trust in him.

Proclaiming Christ
Today

In the New Testament church, the process
for an unbeliever to join the church was
three-fold: evangelism, conversion, then
baptism. Today, the usual order in the church
is baptism, evanglization, and then conversion. A major reason why the order was
changed had to do with infant deaths. In the
new order, young children who die before
they are old enough to make a mature decision to turn to Jesus are still under God's
grace and given every hope of eternal life.
This change does not mean that evangelization and conversion are no longer necessary

for every individual. As the *Catechism of the Catholic Church* says:

> God "desires all men to be saved and to come to the knowledge of the truth": that is, of Christ Jesus. Christ must be proclaimed to all nations and individuals, so that this revelation may reach to the ends of the earth. (CCC, 74)

Conversion Is a Gift

The proclamation of the Word of God has Christian conversion as its aim: a complete and sincere adherence to Christ and his Gospel through faith. Conversion is a gift of God, a work of the Blessed Trinity. It is the Spirit who opens people's hearts so that they can believe in Christ and "confess him" (see 1 Corinthians 12:3); of those who draw near to him through faith Jesus says: "No one can come to me unless the Father who sent me draws him" (John 6:44).

From the outset, conversion is expressed in faith which is total and radical, and which neither limits nor hinders God's gift. At the same time, it gives rise to a dynamic and lifelong process which demands a continual turning away from "life according to the flesh" to "life according to the

Spirit" (see Romans 8:3-13). Conversion means accepting, by a personal decision, the saving sovereignty of Christ and becoming his disciple.

(Pope John Paul II: Mission of the Redeemer, December 7, 1990, 46)